DEDICATION

To my children, Faith, Calvin, and Tyson. May you remember that your feelings are just part of the experience on this Earth journey. Just allow them!

My Magical Feelings
The Magic of Me Series

www.authorbcummings.com

ISBN: 978-1-951597-17-7 (hardcover)
ISBN: 978-1-951597-46-7 (paperback)
ISBN: 978-1-951597-18-4 (ebook)

Library of Congress Control Number: 2021908165

Illustrations by Nejla Shojaie
Editing by Laura Boffa, Tamara Ritterrshaus, Sam Pendleton

Printed in the USA
Signature Book Printing

First printing edition 2021.

Free Kids Press

FREE
KIDS
PRESS

THE MAGIC OF ME
MY MAGICAL FEELINGS

WRITTEN BY
BECKY CUMMINGS

ILLUSTRATED BY
NEJLA SHOJAIE

Knock-knock, who's at the heart door?

"Feelings here, to help you explore!"

Like crayons coloring you within,

all the rainbow colors join in.

Listen closely to this life advice,

don't sort feelings, bad or nice.

Tell your feelings it's okay

to color life a magical way.

Hearing names or words that hurt,

getting teased about your shirt.

Saying bye to furry friends.

The final day when summer ends.

I feel sad and that's okay!

POOL
CLOSED

Eating cones of cold ice cream.

Waking up from a happy dream.

Building castles made of sand.

Giving friends a helping hand.

I feel joy and that's okay!

Mom and Dad are busy today,
Sister has no time to play.
Brother wants to use the phone.
Spending recess all alone.

I feel lonely and that's okay!

Asked to join a friend's birthday.

Grown-ups listen to what you say.

Wear a jersey, playing ball.

Someone helps you when you fall.

I feel accepted and that's okay!

Put to bed too early one night.

People using words to fight.

A plate of food that you don't like.

Someone breaks your brand-new bike.

I feel **angry** and that's okay!

Grandma plays your favorite game.

Your friend and you dress up the same.

Kitty purrs and doggy kisses.

Someone sweet that grants your wishes.

I feel **loved** and that's okay!

Having trouble with the glue,

fall off your bike, can't tie your shoe.

Make mistakes and apologize,

lots of tears fall from your eyes.

I feel **embarrassed** and that's okay!

Reading, writing, speaking thoughts,
teaching others what you've been taught.
Using all your gifts and mind
to dream big dreams for human-kind!

I feel **smart** and that's okay!

Waking from a scary dream,

chased by bugs, that made you scream.

Getting lost inside a store.

Swimming far away from shore.

I feel scared and that's okay!

Mommy holds you super tight,

bedtime snuggles in the night.

Learn and laugh with kids at school.

Family picnics by the pool.

I feel safe and that's okay!

Back to school you start a new grade.

Speaking about something you made.

Meeting people when you're out.

Wanting to whisper when asked to shout.

I feel **shy** and that's okay!

Flip or dive into a lake.

Use a recipe to cook or bake.

Step on stage and dance or sing.

In the batter's box, you take a swing.

I feel **bold** and that's okay!

Honor feelings, breathe them deep.

What comes will go, they aren't to keep.

So laugh or cry

and know it's okay

to feel your feelings your own magic way!

YOUR PICTURE HERE!

TIPS FOR HELPING CHILDREN WITH THEIR FEELINGS

1. When children are having a strong emotion, help them name the feeling, remind them it's okay, and allow them to experience it. We tend to want to prevent our children from having certain experiences by instantly fixing things, but it is important for them to explore a variety of feelings in a safe way. For example, if a child forgets to bring homework to school, he may feel embarrassed. Instead of driving it to school to prevent that emotion, allow the child to have the experience.

2. Read each verse to your child and have them repeat the 'I statement' after you.

3. Teach your children coping strategies to improve their mood if they do not enjoy how they are feeling. More details can be found in *My Magical Moods*, book six in The Magic of Me Series.

ENJOY MORE BOOKS IN THIS SERIES BY BECKY CUMMINGS!

THE MAGIC OF ME
MY MAGICAL WORDS
WRITTEN BY BECKY CUMMINGS
ILLUSTRATED BY ZUZANA SVOBODOVÁ

THE MAGIC OF ME
MY MAGICAL CHOICES
WRITTEN BY BECKY CUMMINGS
ILLUSTRATED BY ZUZANA SVOBODOVÁ

THE MAGIC OF ME
MY MAGICAL DREAMS
WRITTEN BY BECKY CUMMINGS
ILLUSTRATED BY ZUZANA SVOBODOVÁ

THE MAGIC OF ME
MY MAGICAL GIFTS
WRITTEN BY BECKY CUMMINGS
ILLUSTRATED BY ZUZANA SVOBODOVÁ

THE MAGIC OF ME
MY MAGICAL FOODS
WRITTEN BY BECKY CUMMINGS
ILLUSTRATED BY ZUZANA SVOBODOVÁ

BECKY CUMMINGS
The MAGIC of ME
A KID'S GUIDE TO CREATING HAPPINESS

for older readers 8-12

www.authorbcummings.com